CLASSIC ROCK FOR TWO

Arrangements by Peter Deneff

ISBN 978-1-5400-6544-5

HAL•LEONARD®

Visit Hal Leonard Online at
www.halleonard.com

Contact Us:
Hal Leonard
7777 West Bluemound Road
Milwaukee, WI 53213
Email: info@halleonard.com

In Europe contact:
Hal Leonard Europe Limited
42 Wigmore Street
Marylebone, London, W1U 2RN
Email: info@halleonardeurope.com

In Australia contact:
Hal Leonard Australia Pty. Ltd.
4 Lentara Court
Cheltenham, Victoria, 3192 Australia
Email: info@halleonard.com.au

BANG A GONG
(Get It On)

TROMBONES

Words and Music by
MARC BOLAN

21
25
28
32
36
39

CAN'T FIGHT THIS FEELING

TROMBONES

Words and Music by
KEVIN CRONIN

21
25
29
33
37
40
rit.
rit.

CARRY ON WAYWARD SON

TROMBONES

Words and Music by
KERRY LIVGREN

21
25
29
33
37
41

COLD AS ICE

TROMBONES

Words and Music by MICK JONES
and LOU GRAMM

Medium Rock shuffle

22
26
31
35
39
43

COME ON EILEEN

TROMBONES

Words and Music by KEVIN ROWLAND,
JAMES PATTERSON and KEVIN ADAMS

21
25
29
33
37
40

COME TOGETHER

TROMBONES

Words and Music byJOHN LENNON
and PAUL McCARTNEY

23
28
33
38
43
48

CROCODILE ROCK

TROMBONES

Words and Music by ELTON JOHN
and BERNIE TAUPIN

21
25
29
32
36
40

DOWN ON THE CORNER

TROMBONES

Words and Music by
JOHN FOGERTY

26
31
36
42
47
52

EVERY LITTLE THING SHE DOES IS MAGIC

TROMBONES

Words and Music by
STING

26
31
37
43
47
1.
51
2.

FREE FALLIN'

TROMBONES

Words and Music by TOM PETTY
and JEFF LYNNE

28
33
38
44
49
54

HURTS SO GOOD

TROMBONES

Words and Music by JOHN MELLENCAMP
and GEORGE GREEN

22
26
To Coda
30
34
38
42
D.S. al Coda
CODA

THE JOKER

TROMBONES

Words and Music by STEVE MILLER,
EDDIE CURTIS and AHMET ERTEGUN

26
31
35
39
43
47
1.
2.

LIVIN' ON A PRAYER

TROMBONES

Words and Music byJON BON JOVI,
DESMOND CHILD and RICHIE SAMBORA

To Coda
1.
2.
D.S. al Coda
CODA

MAGGIE MAY

TROMBONES

Words and Music by ROD STEWART
and MARTIN QUITTENTON

Moderately

21
25
29
33
38
43

MR. ROBOTO

TROMBONES

Words and Music by
DENNIS DeYOUNG

19
Play 3 times
22
25
28
31
1.
2.

MONEY FOR NOTHING

TROMBONES

Words and Music by MARK KNOPFLER
and STING

Moderate Rock

16
19
22
25
28
1.
2.

ONE MORE NIGHT

TROMBONES

Words and Music by
PHIL COLLINS

30
36
42
48
54
60

PEACE OF MIND

TROMBONES

Words and Music by
TOM SCHOLZ

21
24
27
30
33
36

REELING IN THE YEARS

TROMBONES

Words and Music by WALTER BECKER
and DONALD FAGEN

16
19
22
25
28
1.
2.

SMOKE ON THE WATER

TROMBONES

Words and Music by RITCHIE BLACKMORE,
IAN GILLAN, ROGER GLOVER,
JON LORD and IAN PAICE

26
To Coda
31
1.
2.
36
41
45
D.S. al Coda
CODA
1.
2.

SUMMER OF '69

TROMBONES

Words and Music by BRYAN ADAMS
and JIM VALLANCE

21
25
29
33
D.C. al Coda
CODA
36
40

UPTOWN GIRL

TROMBONES

Words and Music by
BILLY JOEL

26
32
37
42
48
53

YOU'RE THE INSPIRATION

TROMBONES

Words and Music by PETER CETERA
and DAVID FOSTER

21
25
29
33
36
39

HAL LEONARD PRESENTS

EASY INSTRUMENTAL DUETS

Start your duet playing experience with these fun songbooks! Over 20 easy duet arrangements for two instrumentalists are featured in each of these collections. Woodwind and brass editions can be played together as can the string editions. **Only $9.99 each!**

THE BEATLES FOR TWO

23 favorites from the Fab Four in easy duet arrangements for two instrumentalists are featured in this collection: All You Need Is Love • Eleanor Rigby • Here Comes the Sun • Hey Jude • I Want to Hold Your Hand • Penny Lane • Something • Yellow Submarine • Yesterday • and more.

00291024	FLUTE	00291028	TROMBONE
00291025	CLARINET	00291029	VIOLIN
00291026	ALTO SAX	00291030	CELLO
00291027	TRUMPET		

BROADWAY SONGS FOR TWO

22 showstoppers: Any Dream Will Do • Bring Him Home • Cabaret • Edelweiss • For Forever • Hello, Dolly! • I Believe • Memory • One • Popular • Seasons of Love • Seventy Six Trombones • Tomorrow • Where Is Love? • You've Got a Friend • and more.

00252493	FLUTE	00252497	TROMBONE
00252494	CLARINET	00252500	VIOLIN
00252495	ALTO SAX	00252501	CELLO
00252496	TRUMPET		

CHRISTMAS CAROLS FOR TWO

Songs include: Angels We Have Heard on High • Away in a Manger • Deck the Hall • Jingle Bells • Joy to the World • O Holy Night • Silent Night • We Wish You a Merry Christmas • and more.

00277964	FLUTE	00277968	TROMBONE
00277965	CLARINET	00277969	VIOLIN
00277966	ALTO SAX	00277970	CELLO
00277967	TRUMPET		

HAL•LEONARD®

CHRISTMAS HITS FOR TWO

22 terrific holiday duets: All I Want for Christmas Is You • Baby, It's Cold Outside • The Christmas Song (Chestnuts Roasting on an Open Fire) • Do You Want to Build a Snowman? • Feliz Navidad • Have Yourself a Merry Little Christmas • It's Beginning to Look like Christmas • Let It Snow! Let It Snow! Let It Snow! • Mary, Did You Know? • Rockin' Around the Christmas Tree • Silver Bells • White Christmas • and more.

00172461	FLUTE	00172465	TROMBONE
00172462	CLARINET	00172466	VIOLIN
00172463	ALTO SAX	00172467	CELLO
00172464	TRUMPET		

CLASSIC ROCK FOR TWO

23 classic rock songs: Bang a Gong (Get It On) · Can't Fight This Feeling · Carry on Wayward Son · Cold As Ice · Come on Eileen · Come Together · Crocodile Rock · Down on the Corner · Every Little Thing She Does Is Magic · Free Fallin' · Hurts So Good · The Joker · Livin' on a Prayer · and more.

00303026	FLUTE	00303030	TROMBONE
00303027	CLARINET	00303031	VIOLIN
00303028	ALTO SAX	00303032	CELLO
00303029	TRUMPET		

CLASSICAL THEMES FOR TWO

24 favorite melodies from top classical composers: Air on the G String • Blue Danube Waltz • Canon in D • Eine Kleine Nachtmusik • Hallelujah Chorus • Jesu, Joy of Man's Desiring • Minuet in G Major • Ode to Joy • Pictures at an Exhibition • Sheep May Safely Graze • Trumpet Voluntary • William Tell Overture • and more.

00254439	FLUTE	00254443	TROMBONE
00254440	CLARINET	00254444	VIOLIN
00254441	ALTO SAX	00254445	CELLO
00254442	TRUMPET		

Prices, contents and availability subject to change without notice. Sales restrictions to some countries apply. All prices listed in U.S. funds.

DISNEY SONGS FOR TWO

23 Disney favorites: Beauty and the Beast • Circle of Life • Evermore • Friend Like Me • How Far I'll Go • Let It Go • Mickey Mouse March • Supercalifragilisticexpialidocious • When You Wish upon a Star • A Whole New World • Zip-A-Dee-Doo-Dah • and more.

00284643	FLUTE	00284647	TROMBONE
00284644	CLARINET	00284648	VIOLIN
00284645	ALTO SAX	00284649	CELLO
00284646	TRUMPET		

HIT SONGS FOR TWO

22 mega hits: All About That Bass • All of Me • Brave • Can't Stop the Feeling • Grenade • Hey, Soul Sister • I Will Wait • Let Her Go • 100 Years • Royals • Shake It Off • Shape of You • Stay with Me • Viva La Vida • and more.

00252482	FLUTE	00252486	TROMBONE
00252483	CLARINET	00252487	VIOLIN
00252484	ALTO SAX	00252488	CELLO
00252485	TRUMPET		

MOVIE SONGS FOR TWO

23 blockbuster hits are featured in this collection: City of Stars • Footloose • Hallelujah • Moon River • The Pink Panther • Puttin' on the Ritz • Skyfall • That's Amore • and more.

00284651	FLUTE	00284655	TROMBONE
00284652	CLARINET	00284656	VIOLIN
00284653	ALTO SAX	00284657	CELLO
00284654	TRUMPET		

POP CLASSICS FOR TWO

23 classic pop hits: Africa · Alone · Can't Smile Without You · Centerfold · Dancing Queen · Dust in the Wind · Every Breath You Take · Eye of the Tiger · I Melt with You · I Still Haven't Found What I'm Looking For · Imagine · Jessie's Girl · and more.

00303019	FLUTE	00303023	TROMBONE
00303020	CLARINET	00303024	VIOLIN
00303021	ALTO SAX	00303025	CELLO
00303022	TRUMPET		

ORDER TODAY FROM YOUR FAVORITE MUSIC RETAILER AT **HALLEONARD.COM**

1119
508